How to plant a room and grow a happy home.

Morgan Doane and Erin Harding
of _House Plant Club_

How to plant a room and grow a happy home.

Laurence King

LAURENCE KING

First published in Great Britain in 2022
by Laurence King, an imprint of
The Orion Publishing Group Ltd
Carmelite House, 50 Victoria
Embankment, London EC4Y 0DZ

An Hachette UK Company

10 9 8 7 6 5 4 3 2 1

A CIP catalogue record for this book is
available from the British Library.

ISBN 978-0-8578-2906-1

Design: Masumi Briozzo

Origination by F1 Colour, UK
Printed in China by Prosperous Printing Co. Ltd

Laurence King is committed to ethical and
sustainable production. We are proud
participants in the Book Chain Project®.
bookchainproject.com

**BOOK
CHAIN
PROJECT**

www.laurenceking.com
www.orionbooks.co.uk

Contents

Introduction

When we wrote our first book, *How to raise a plant and make it love you back*, we wanted to introduce some of our favorite house plants to a wide audience by showing how easy it can be to raise plants at home and to keep them happy. Since then, enthusiasm for house plants has continued to grow and we welcome new folks into the House Plant Club each and every day. If collecting and caring for plants is something you enjoy, you may want to start there. But if you, like us, enjoy taking things a step further, then this book is the obvious next step.

Here we've outlined some fun and easy projects that will take your plant collection to the next level. We are building on the basic ideas in our first book and the same rules apply. Make sure you have the right plants for the right rooms and assess your lighting situation before deciding where to house your project. But once you have those things under control, the sky is the limit for what you can do to create well-planted rooms throughout the year and throughout your home.

Though we've outlined instructions for the specific plants we've shown, you should feel free to customize and personalize the projects to your heart's content. They should be personal and unique to your home and house plant collection. For example, if you can't find the specific plant we use in a project but you have something similar in mind, go for it. We've tried to show each project with variation possibilities where we could but let your imagination run wild when you start making projects for your own home. And most of all, have fun!

Erin and Morgan

We all know that water is essential to keeping plants alive, but it is usually dispensed and forgotten as it disappears into the soil. The following projects bring water to the forefront and allow us to see things that are normally hidden from view.

WORKING WITH WATER

Propagation display

RHAPHIDOPHORA TETRASPERMA
MONSTERA ADANSONII

Plant propagation is the process of making new plants from existing plants. There are a variety of ways to propagate but our favorite is water propagation. Water propagation allows you to see the roots form and grow, whereas with soil propagation you can grow new plants but you can't watch the progress.

The beautiful thing about water propagation is the ability to display propagating plants as decor in the home. A variety of vessels can be used to water propagate. Whether you use old canning jars, test tubes, or vases, propagating plants will make a stunning addition to the rest of your decor. We suggest using a variety of plants grouped together to create a propagation bouquet. Get creative and have fun!

Supplies

· Plant to propagate

· Clean glass vessel

· Room-temperature water

· Clean scissors, knife, or gardening snips

RHAPHIDOPHORA TETRASPERMA
PILEA PEPEROMIOIDES
EPIPREMNUM AUREUM
CHLOROPHYTUM COMOSUM

How to water propagate

Steps

1. Locate the correct place on the plant to cut. Many plants have a root node on the stem, usually located opposite a leaf. Cut the stem approximately ¼" (6mm) below the root node.

2. Remove the leaf at that spot. Place the cutting in the vessel with room-temperature water. Ensure the water line is covering the root node area. Depending on the plant, roots should form in 1–2 weeks.

<u>Care</u>

Water

Replace the water as needed throughout the root growth time. It is safe to keep plants in water as long as the leaves look healthy and the roots remain a cream color. Signs of needing to remove a plant from water include yellowing or falling of leaves and brown or black roots. Plants can be transferred to soil when roots are a minimum of 2-4 inches (5-10cm) long (for best results).

Light

Keep water propagating plants in an area with bright light for at least 4 hours per day.

PROPAGATE A VARIETY OF PLANTS TO CREATE THE SENSE OF LIVING DECOR.

PHILODENDRON HEDERACEUM

Forcing bulbs in water

Having lived through winters in cold climates, we can attest that there is nothing quite like seeing the first signs of spring outdoors. When the tulips and daffodils start poking out of the ground, we all know that better weather is on the way and we will soon have beautiful blooms in our gardens. The joy that spring flowers bring can be replicated in your home very easily with just a little planning and know-how.

Choosing a container

You could use a specialist bulb vase, with a cup at the top to cradle the base of the bulb while the roots extend into the water. But you're not limited to this sort of vase; you can use containers of other shapes or sizes. Finding the right glass jar is half the fun of this project. Look for a vessel with visual interest, such as curves or colored glass that goes well with your decor. Depending on the vessel you choose, you might need to add a substrate to keep the bulb or bulbs from sinking to the bottom. You can use rocks, small pebbles, or decorative glass beads to create visual interest. As the roots begin to grow and seek out the water, they will intertwine with the substrate and you'll have a cool little science experiment on display.

TULIP BULBS

Choosing plants

The trickiest thing about water-forcing bulbs is knowing whether the bulb you have has been chilled or not. You can purchase pre-chilled bulbs—just make sure to ask, if they aren't labeled. You can also buy bulbs in the fall and chill them yourself. To do this, place the bulbs in a dry paper bag and store them in a cold garage or attic for 12-15 weeks for the cold to activate the bulbs. Once they have a bit of a green sprout up top, you can begin the water-forcing.

We have had success with forcing the following bulbs in water:

· Amaryllis
· Paperwhite narcissi
· Tulips
· Daffodils
· Hyacinth

NARCISSUS PAPYRACEUS BULBS

Supplies

· Glass container

· Dry or potted bulb(s)

· Room-temperature water

· Rocks, pebbles, or glass beads (optional)

TULIP BULB
DAFFODIL BULBS

Tip

If you love the look of water-forced bulbs, you can always buy potted plants and transfer them to your favorite glass vessel. This allows you to skip the chilling and go straight to the gorgeous blooming stage. Look for healthy bulbs with undamaged foliage. If the flower buds are already visible, it won't take long for them to bloom once you get them home and transfer them to water.

HYACINTH BULB

Steps

1. Wash the container thoroughly with soap and water and allow to dry.

2. Fill the vessel with room-temperature water (see Care), then position the rocks, pebbles, or beads (if using) to support the bulb or bulbs.

3. If you are using potted bulbs, carefully remove them from the soil mix and rinse bulb and roots with room-temperature water. Run your fingers through the roots to remove as much soil as possible. If the roots are longer than about 2 inches (5cm), you can trim them with clean, sharp scissors to allow them to fit your vessel.

4. Carefully place the bulbs in the container, roots down, so that they are supported either by the stones or by the neck of the jar.

Care

Water

It's important to keep the water topped up, so that your bulbs don't dry out. The ideal water level is just below the base of the bulb, where the roots emerge, so that the bulb itself is hardly touching the water. Should the water ever become murky, you can replace it completely with fresh water. Given the short lifespan of fresh blooms, this may not be necessary during the season.

Have you run out of windowsill space? Or do you need a way to keep your house plants away from curious children or playful pets? Consider using one of these innovative hanging projects to put plants on a new level within your home.

HANGING PLANTS

Kokedama

Kokedama originated in Japan and are admired by plant enthusiasts around the globe as a unique and beautiful way to display plants. Kokedama is essentially a sphere-shaped, moss-wrapped plant. What makes this a fun piece of living decor is its ability to be either hung or displayed in a stand or dish. A single kokedama can make a gorgeous statement piece, but grouped together they can add whimsy to any room.

Choosing plants

A variety of plants can be used to create kokedama. For beginner plant parents, we recommend using *Epipremnum aureum* (commonly known as Pothos or Devil's Ivy) or jungle cacti (such as *Rhipsalis* or *Epiphyllum*), which are a little more forgiving. If you're a seasoned plant parent, try *Begonia*, ferns, or even *Anthurium*.

Supplies

· Peat moss

· Bonsai soil mix

· Mixing bowl or dish

· Plant

· Sheet moss or forged moss

· Fishing line

AGLAONEMA SP. KOKEDAMA
TRADESCANTIA SP. KOKEDAMA
MONSTERA SP. KOKEDAMA

23

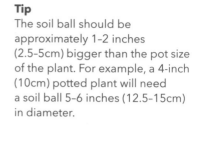

Tip
The soil ball should be approximately 1–2 inches (2.5–5cm) bigger than the pot size of the plant. For example, a 4-inch (10cm) potted plant will need a soil ball 5–6 inches (12.5–15cm) in diameter.

Steps

1. Combine equal parts peat moss and bonsai soil mix in the mixing bowl or dish.

2. Pour water into the mix to create a clay-like substance.

3. Form the mix into a ball shape (for the appropriate size, see Tip). The ball should be able to stay together on its own. Set to one side.

4. Remove the plant from its pot and gently rub excess soil from the roots. Set to one side.

5. Carefully break the soil ball in half.

6. Place the root ball of the plant between the two halves and re-form the soil around it into a ball.

7. Wrap the sheet or forged moss around the soil ball, covering the entire ball.

8. Wrap the fishing line around the moss ball once and tie off with a double knot. Without cutting the fishing line, continue wrapping it tightly around the ball, over and over (in different directions) to secure the moss. Tie the fishing line off with a double knot and cut off the excess.

9. If you want to hang your kokedama, make a loop in one end of a long piece of fishing line and tie it to the kokedama.

BEGONIA 'RIVER NILE'

KOKEDAMA ENLIVEN ANY SPACE AND MAKE IT FEEL MORE CONNECTED TO NATURE.

<u>Care</u>

The type of plant you use will determine the amount of light your kokedama will need. Research the specific plant and care for it accordingly. Kokedama that are properly looked after can last for a few years before they need refreshing with new soil and binding in a bigger moss ball.

Water

The first few weeks are crucial, so use this time to get to know your plant and determine the best frequency of watering. It's a good idea to learn how to recognize signs of thirst. If the plant is displaying curled, droopy, or brown-edged leaves, or even losing leaves entirely, it's probably time to water. Soak the kokedama in a bowl of room-temperature water for 20-30 minutes—just long enough for it to soak up water through the moss and into the soil. Remove it from the water and squeeze to release excess water. Once it has stopped dripping, the kokedama can be placed back on display.

Fertilizer

Just like other house plants, kokedama need nutrients to thrive. Supplementing with plant food can help yours grow big and beautiful. We like to use a liquid fertilizer in the soaking water in the spring and summer, following the directions on the package.

Hanging air plant driftwood display

Air plants are a gorgeous, low-maintenance way to bring plants into your home. Typically, they are simply displayed on their own in a dish or perhaps as a collection on a table. But with a little time and a few materials, they can be transformed into a piece of living art. Bring the outdoors in and show off your creativity by making this fun air plant project using an organic material such as driftwood for the base. This piece can be created on a small or large scale. Small-scale pieces are great for an apartment or office, while larger designs can be displayed above a sofa or suspended over a dining table. Another striking option is to arrange several small pieces in a geometric pattern on the wall. Given all the air plant varieties and organic mounting materials, such as cork bark, driftwood, cedar boards, and cholla wood, the display options are vast. The beauty of this project is that it can be hung just about anywhere. Whether you hang it on the wall or from the ceiling, it is sure to be noticed.

Air plants

Tillandsia is a genus of approximately 600 species in the Bromeliaceae family, more commonly known as air plants. It gets its nickname from the plants' ability to pull the water and nutrients they need from the air around them, via trichomes (specialized growths) on their leaves. Air plants use roots at their base to attach themselves to bark, rock, and other plants. They can grow easily inside the home, and with proper care they will not only bloom, but will also produce pups (offshoots) that can eventually become self-sufficient plants. For this project, select a variety of air plants to show off the myriad shapes, sizes, colors, and textures that are available. This will help you to create a beautiful organic look. Air plants can be found at your local plant store, online, and even at some grocery stores.

TILLANDSIA IONANTHA
TILLANDSIA XEROGRAPHICA

Common varieties

Tillandsia xerographica
Tillandsia ionantha
Tillandsia stricta
Tillandsia capitata
Tillandsia bulbosa

Supplies

· Air plants

· Moss (reserved fresh moss)

· Fishing line or floral wire

· Driftwood or similar base material

· Waterproof, non-toxic adhesive
  (optional)

· Drill and drill bit

· String

· Hook or nail, for hanging

Steps

1. Wrap the base of each air plant with a small amount of moss. Secure the moss by wrapping the fishing line or floral wire around the base a few times, and finish off with a double knot. Cut off any excess fishing line or wire.

2. Arrange the moss-wrapped air plants on your base material until you are happy with the result.

3. Secure the moss-wrapped air plants to the base. Either drop a small amount of adhesive on to the moss and hold it firmly against the base until dry, or use fishing line or floral wire to tie the moss-wrapped air plants to the base, then secure with a double knot.

4. Where needed, drill holes in the base in order to hang your living art for display. Thread string through the holes and tie to secure.

5. The air plant display can hang from the ceiling or the wall. Use the necessary hardware, and follow the package instructions to hang.

TILLANDSIA IONANTHA
TILLANDSIA XEROGRAPHICA

31

Care

Water

Soak the completed display in a tub or bowl of room-temperature water for approximately 30 minutes. Remove the display from the water, gently tap off the excess, and allow it to dry. Whenever possible, air plants should be dried upside down, to allow water to drain from the cupped bases and curved leaves.

The key to proper watering is getting to know your air plants so that you can see when they require watering. Instead of sticking to a schedule, look out for curling or even browning tips and wrinkled leaves, and water as needed.

Light

This display will do best in an area of bright filtered light, but if your room doesn't have that, be sure to allow your creation as much light as possible. The most important thing to remember is that the amount of light will dictate the frequency with which you'll need to water. The more light the air plants get, the thirstier they will be. If your creation is receiving lower light, you will water less often.

TILLANDSIA IONANTHA
TILLANDSIA ARGENTEA

TILLANDSIA BUTZII
TILLANDSIA CAPITATA
TILLANDSIA IONANTHA

Modern beaded
plant hanger

For decades plant hangers have been made in homes around the world. While they have gone in and out of fashion through the years, they're back now and can be customized in countless ways. Hanging plants in the home is not only beautiful and stylish, but also a great way to keep plants out of reach of children and pets. We love this project because it's so easy—you don't need to learn how to tie a bunch of knots to make something that looks really great. The best part about it is that there's no right way. Get creative with your beading to produce the look you want!

Variations

Here we show just one way to make a modern beaded plant hanger, but there are many variations to this project. We used 3-mm macramé cord, but you could opt for hemp rope, string, or yarn instead. The length of the plant hanger can be adjusted to fit your needs. Here we show you how to make a plant hanger that is approximately 36 inches (90cm) long from the top of the wooden ring to the bottom of the fringe. It will happily accommodate pots up to 6 inches (15cm) in diameter.

Wooden beads like the ones we use here can be found at craft stores or online. Be aware of the bead size and hole opening, since the bead must fit easily over the six strands of cord. Another way to customize your hanger would be to paint or stain the beads instead of leaving them their natural color—this way they could be matched to your home decor. The possibilities are endless!

HOYA CARNOSA 'TRICOLOR'
RHAPHIDOPHORA TETRASPERMA
TILLANDSIA XEROGRAPHICA

Steps

1. Cut three pieces of macramé cord, each 72 inches (1.8m) long.

2. Take the three pieces of cord and fold them in half. Pass the folded middle section through a large wooden ring.

3. Pull the ends of the cord through the cord loop you've created. The wooden ring will be the hanger at the top.

4. Begin threading the wooden beads and rings on to the cord in a random order (or make a plan for a pattern). The beads and rings should only occupy the top 10 inches (25cm) of the cord.

Supplies

· Macramé cord

· Wooden craft rings in various sizes, plus one large ring for the hanger

· Wooden craft beads in various sizes

5. Once you've achieved the look you want, add one more bead or ring and secure it with a knot to hold everything in place.

6. Approximately 16–18 inches (40–46cm) from the last knot, add one more bead or ring and tie a knot underneath to secure it. The pot will sit on top of this knot. You should have a few inches of cord remaining at the bottom.

7. To add your pot, spread out the six pieces of macramé cord and place it in the middle. Be sure that the cords are evenly spaced around the pot so that they hold it in place.

HOYA CARNOSA 'TRICOLOR'
RHAPHIDOPHORA TETRASPERMA
TILLANDSIA XEROGRAPHICA

Don't have room for a full-size conservatory or greenhouse in your home? Don't worry. These fun-size projects pair plants with glass in ways that allow you to display them throughout your home, no matter how limited the space may be.

PLANTS IN GLASS

Terrariums

These gorgeous self-sustaining environments inside sealed containers are a fun project for adults and kids alike. A variety of materials, such as rocks, moss, and sticks, can be used to create the perfect landscape that will last indefinitely, with the proper care.

Choosing a container

For a terrarium to work properly, it should be made of glass—so that the plants get enough light—and it must have a sealed lid, so that all moisture stays inside the container. Cork and screw-on lids both create a good seal, but other materials will work too. If you use a screw-on lid, poke a small hole in it to release pressure inside the container. Terrariums can be made in a variety of sizes. Spice jars, test tubes, and baby-food jars can be used for miniature terrariums, while aquariums and carboys (demijohns) can be used to create larger versions. Finding the container is half the fun!

Plants for terrariums

The best plants for terrariums are tropical, slower-growing plants that come from very humid environments. It's important to choose your container first, then decide which size of plant works best for the space you have. Our favorite terrarium plants are:

Hypoestes (Polka Dot Plant)
Peperomia varieties
Fittonia (Nerve Plant)
Begonia varieties
ferns
Epipremnum aureum
Maranta leuconeura (Prayer Plant)
mosses

PILEA MICROPHYLLA VARIEGATA

Steps

1. Place about 1 inch (2.5cm) of horticultural charcoal (depending on the size of your terrarium) in the bottom of the container. This layer is vital in a closed terrarium, because it helps to prevent the growth of bacteria and improves drainage. If your container has a narrow neck, you may need to use a funnel to add the charcoal.

2. Next, add the soil, using a funnel if necessary. The amount will vary depending on the size of your container and of the root balls of your chosen plants. The layer must be thick enough for the roots to have room to grow. We suggest allowing for 1 inch (2.5cm) of growth.

Tip

It's important to select plants and materials that will fit easily into your container. Err on the side of smaller plants, so they have room to grow.

Supplies

· Horticultural charcoal

· Sealable glass container

· Soil

· Plants

· Rocks in various sizes

· Other materials for designing and decorating (bark, sticks, small animal figurines, etc.)

· Spray bottle of water

· Scissors, long tweezers, or chopsticks for manipulating items

· Funnel (optional; for adding material to a narrow-necked container)

3. Place the plants in the container and arrange them on top of the soil, using scissors, tweezers, or chopsticks if necessary. Taller or faster-growing plants should be toward the back, while mosses and slower-growing plants do best in the front.

4. Add another layer of soil to cover the roots of the plants completely.

5. Now it's time to design! Use rock, bark, and any other materials you like to create your beautiful ecosystem.

6. Once the terrarium is to your liking, spray the inside walls with water. This will help to clear the container of debris and give the plants their first drink.

7. Seal the terrarium with the lid.

Care

Light

Place your terrarium in an area with bright indirect light. The light and heat from the sun create moisture inside the terrarium; it will evaporate, and water droplets will condense on the inside surfaces of the container. The condensation rolls down the side of the jar, creating a water source for the plants. This cycle can continue indefinitely. It's important to note that you may need to move your terrarium around at first to find the perfect spot where it gets enough light to create condensation, without the glass getting too hot. As with other plants, terrariums should be turned from time to time, to allow even growth and hydration inside.

Maintenance

Open the terrarium for a couple of minutes every few months to give it a bit of fresh air. If any plants turn brown or die, remove them. Routinely trim plants that are outgrowing the container. If a week goes by with no condensation forming inside your terrarium, open the container and give the sides a good spray of water. Seal the lid up, and place in an area with brighter light.

EXPERIMENT WITH SCALE: TRY SEVERAL SMALL TERRARIUMS OR ONE LARGE ONE TO MAKE AN IMPACT.

Open terrarium

Creating a tiny landscape of your favorite outdoor space is not only a meditative project— its beauty can last for years. The landscape is created by layering materials in a glass container and complementing those layers with plants. Each layer serves a purpose, and together they make a healthy and beautiful place for your plants to live. True terrariums are closed glass structures that are self-sustaining (see page 43). Open terrariums are created in a similar way, but they are not self-sustaining, meaning regular watering and care are needed. The openness allows you to create tropical or arid landscapes in a beautiful glass container while maintaining air circulation and access to the plants.

Choosing a container

As with closed terrariums, one of the fun parts of this project is choosing a glass container. Whether it's a recycled pickle jar or a hand-blown glass vessel, there is a container to suit every style. We highly recommend using a container you have on hand, or finding one at a second-hand store. Choose the container first, so that you are able to select plants that fit it perfectly.

PEPEROMIA RUBY CASCADE
PEPEROMIA CAPERATA 'RASPBERRY RIPPLE'
PEPEROMIA 'PICCOLO BANDA'

Choosing plants

A wide variety of plants can be used, but you'll need to choose species that will fit comfortably inside your container. You can always take cuttings from plants you already have, or purchase smaller plants from your local plant store.

To allow you to care for your creation properly, choose plants that need similar conditions. For example, if you are going for a tropical feel, you could combine a small *Monstera adansonii* with a *Peperomia caperata* and *Chamaedorea elegans*. For a desert landscape, you could include *Euphorbia*, along with *Opuntia* (Prickly Pear) and *Mammillaria* cacti. You can also create a jungle look with epiphytes (plants that grow on other plants and trees in their natural environment) such as *Rhipsalis*, *Hoya*, and *Platycerium* (Staghorn Fern).

Tip
The amount of material you use will depend on your container. The bigger the container, the thicker the layers of material should be, but they should take up no more than half of the depth of the container. Be sure to include enough soil for your plants to root into.

Supplies

- Glass container
- Small lava rock
- Horticultural charcoal
- Potting soil
- Plants
- Scissors, tweezers, chopsticks, etc., depending on the shape and height of your container
- Assorted river rock and/or other decorative rocks

Steps

1. Wash the container with soap and warm water.

2. Place a layer of small lava rock in the bottom of the container. This will help with drainage and add a layer of visual interest.

3. Spread a thin layer of horticultural charcoal on top of the lava rock. Charcoal helps with a variety of things, including drainage, moisture control, and bacteria prevention. It is not absolutely necessary to use it in an open container, but we like to add a layer to assist with drainage.

4. Add a layer of potting soil. The amount will vary depending on the size of your plants and container (see Tip).

5. Remove the plants from their pots and rub any excess soil from the roots. Place the plants in the potting soil, moving them around until you're happy with the look of your container. Use scissors, tweezers, or chopsticks if necessary to make this step easier. Have fun with it!

6. Add more potting soil, as needed, to ensure all the roots are covered.

7. Finally, add decorative rock on top of the soil for a beautiful finishing touch.

<u>Care</u>

The type of care will depend on the plants. Cacti and succulents will need more light and less water; tropical plants might need more frequent watering but may be happy with a slightly shadier situation.

Water
Watering is the trickiest part with any container that does not have a drainage hole. We suggest using a watering can with a small spout. Slowly pour the water into the container for a few seconds at a time, waiting for the water to fully settle in between each pour. Add just enough for the soil to become moist without water pooling at the bottom of the container. Frequency of watering will depend on the plants. We suggest getting to know your plants so you can identify signs of thirst. Another suggestion is to water as soon as the soil becomes dry.

Light
Whether you use arid or tropical plants, it's a good idea to place your terrarium where it will receive bright indirect light.

REX BEGONIA 'HARMONY'S FIRE WOMAN'
CHAMAEDOREA ELEGANS

Aquatic plant display

You'll never have to worry about overwatering this one! Aquatic plants have adapted to living in and around water. We've all seen a gorgeous blooming *Nymphaea* (Water Lily) atop a pond, or a beautifully planted aquarium, but how about creating your very own? Here we're going to show you how to make a simple yet stunning aquatic plant display using a Java Fern. This will be a great start to your aquatic plant journey. Once you become more comfortable with aquatic plants, there are many other types to learn about and create with.

Aquascaping

Aquascaping is the art of designing and creating an aquatic landscape. Underwater gardens can be made using materials such as plants, stones, rock, bark, and even fish. Learning how each plant works and interacts with other materials is key to success, and it can take years to perfect the art.

It is important to note that here we show you how to create and care for a display that does not include other living creatures, such as snails or fish. Java Ferns are compatible with a variety of other plants and fish, but we suggest seeking the advice of an aquarist before adding more living elements.

TILLANDSIA XEROGRAPHICA
MICROSORUM PTEROPUS
TILLANDSIA FASCICULATA TRICOLOR 'GOLDEN TORCH'

Microsorum pteropus, **Java Fern**

Java Ferns are arguably the easiest aquatic plants to care for. There are different variants of the species, each one as beautiful as the next, making Java Ferns a favorite of many. The Java Fern is native to southeast Asia and is found in riverbanks and streams in parts of Malaysia and Thailand. It will happily grow either fully or partially under water. As long as the root system is fully submerged, the foliage can live out of the water.

Java Ferns are epiphytic plants that grow on materials such as bark and rock. Unlike other aquatic plants that are planted in the substrate or soil, a Java Fern's root system needs to be free to attach. For this project, we will show you step by step how to facilitate the attachment of Java Ferns on to lava rock.

Choosing a container

Start small and work your way up to a bigger container. That's how we learned! The container should be bigger in circumference than your plant (there should be 1 inch (2.5cm) extra all around), so that the fern has room to grow. We suggest using glass containers such as vases or small aquariums.

Supplies

· Glass container

· Substrate such as rock or gravel (we prefer bagged aquarium rock, which tends to be cleaner)

· Piece of bark or lava rock

· Rock or gravel (optional; to hold down bark that isn't heavy enough)

· _Microsorum pteropus_ (Java Fern plant; can be bought at most aquarium supply or pet stores)

· Fishing line or very thin twine

· Tap water at room temperature (enough to fill the container)

Steps

1. Wash all the materials thoroughly. The container should be washed with soap and water, rinsed well and dried. The rock and bark must be rinsed thoroughly several times, until the water runs clear.

2. Oftentimes, when you buy a Java Fern pre-packaged at a store, you will see several leaves tied together with black thread. This is normal. Remove the plant from its packaging, keeping the thread in place, and rinse off the plant.

3. Attach the plant to the lava rock with fishing line. It does not have to be super-tight, just secure enough that the fern won't float away.

4. Fill the bottom few inches of the container with substrate.

5. Place the rock and Java Fern in the container.

6. Add more substrate as needed to achieve the look you want, but take care not to cover the roots of the plant.

7. Pour in room-temperature water and you're done!

MICROSORUM PTEROPUS

Care

Browning or yellowing leaves do not have to be a cause for worry right away, because it is natural for leaves to die off and new buds to appear over time. However, if the browning starts to spread throughout the plant, it could very well be a nutrient deficiency. Snip off the browning leaves as close to the rhizome/root area as possible, and use a supplement to give the plant more nutrients.

As the plant grows, it can be trimmed or propagated to keep it in the original container. Java Ferns can be propagated by pulling off plantlets growing from the tips of the leaves, or by dividing at the rhizome. Plantlets look like tiny leaves growing at the very tip of the leaves.

Water

Java Ferns are totally fine to be in room-temperature water. Empty out the old water and replace with new whenever things start to look murky. There are many variables that affect how often the water should be changed, but we find that every week or two is a good starting point.

Light

Java Ferns are able to tolerate a variety of light conditions. They typically do best in moderate lighting, but will do just fine in lower or higher light levels. Natural or artificial light can be used for aquatic plant displays. If the Java Fern is in a room with a window, there should be enough daylight, but LED lights can be used in the absence of natural light.

Supplements

Supplements are a great way to promote the healthy growth of Java Ferns. Most contain nitrogen, phosphate, calcium, magnesium, sulfur, iron, and other elements. Use as directed on the packaging.

ZEPHYRANTHES CANDIDA
MICROSORUM PTEROPUS

The houseplant hobby provides endless opportunities for creativity, innovation, and display. Once you've mastered caring for simple potted plants, consider graduating to a more imaginative presentation by utilizing the vertical space of walls and doorways with these living art displays.

LIVING WALL ART

Mounted wall garden

There is nothing more beautiful than walking through a garden in the springtime, taking in the perfect combination of flowers, plants, and grasses. Or strolling through a forest and seeing a lovely log adorned with moss and plants living in harmony. You can re-create something very similar that will hang beautifully in your home! This mounted wall garden is perfect for just about any space. A combination of plants, moss, and bark is all you need to make a stunning piece of living art.

Choosing plants

Epiphytic plants—those that grow on other plants and trees in their natural environment—are the best to use in a project of this kind because they do not have to be planted in soil. They take the nutrients they need from the host plant and absorb water from rain and the air around them. Below are some suitable epiphytes for a mounted wall garden.

Rhipsalis species
Platycerium species
Hoya species
Tillandsia species
Anthurium species
Monstera species
Orchids
Philodendron species
Bromeliads
Ferns

DAVALLIA FEJEENSIS
RHIPSALIS SP.
BEGONIA SP.
TILLANDSIA SP.

Tip

Combine plants with similar care needs on one mount, to make it easier to look after them collectively. Plants that tend to have plump foliage, such as *Hoya*, *Rhipsalis*, and Bromeliads, work very well together. Those with delicate foliage, including *Monstera*, *Anthurium*, and ferns, will cohabit nicely. Within these groups, choose plants with different shapes, colors, and blooms to create a visually pleasing wall garden.

HOYA WAYETII
DAVALLIA FEJEENSIS

Supplies

- Plants
- Moss (harvested)
- Fishing line
- Cork bark (from a reptile supply store), or tree bark or cedar board
- Craft wire
- Drill with a bit slightly larger than the craft wire
- Nail or wall hook

Steps

1. Remove the plants from their pots and gently massage most of the soil away from the roots.

2. Wrap a layer of moss around the roots of each plant and shape into a rough ball. Secure the moss with a few rounds of fishing line and finish with a double knot. This step allows you to hold the plants more easily as you design, and protects the roots.

3. Lay the piece of bark in front of you and play around with the position of the plants. We suggest using one plant as a focal point, close to the middle, and working the others in around it. It may take you some time to get it just right.

4. Fill the spaces between the plants with moss, to create one large moss bed.

5. Once all the plants are in place and you're happy with the look of your arrangement, wrap fishing line all the way around the moss and bark to secure each plant lightly.

6. Wrap the fishing line around the bottom of the mount once and tie a double knot to secure it. Working your way up and then back down the mount, wrap the fishing line tightly around the entire mount, until all the plants and the moss are secured.

7. To hang your mount on the wall (see Care for where to position it), drill a hole in the top of the mount and thread 1 foot (30cm) of wire through it. Twist the wire together to create a hook. Be sure to use a nail or wall hook that can support the weight of your mount.

Care

Water
Fill a tub or large sink with room-temperature water. Soak the whole mount (plants and bark) in the water for approximately 30 minutes. Remove the mount from the water and allow to dry on a towel until the bark is dry to the touch. It is then safe to hang it back on the wall. Over time, you will get to know your wall garden and be able to spot when it needs to be watered. Until then, the wall garden will most likely need to be watered every 7–10 days in the spring and summer. In the fall and winter, it can go closer to 14 days without being watered.

Light
Hang the mounted wall garden as close to a window as possible. It should ideally receive a minimum of 2–3 hours (and a maximum of 6 hours) of direct sun every day.

Fertilizer
Just like other house plants, the mounted wall garden can be fertilized throughout the spring and summer. Add liquid fertilizer to your soaking water, as directed on the packaging.

RHIPSALIS PRISMATICA
RHIPSALIS PILOCARPA
BROMELIAD SP.
HOYA RETUSA

Framed garden

Have you ever seen those beautiful planted framed gardens and wondered how in the world they are made? Maybe you even tried to create one, but the plants died a few months later. We've been there! They're difficult to water and can be very messy, and if a plant dies it's really tricky to plant another in its place. Here's a solution. We designed this framed garden that you can make yourself to house six 4-inch (10cm) nursery or terracotta pots. This way you can easily remove the plants whenever it's time to water them. Also, you can customize the project by staining or painting the wood.

MONSTERA ADANSONII
MONSTERA SP.
CALATHEA ORBIFOLIA
DAVALLIA FEJEENSIS
ASPLENIUM NIDUS
SENECIO PEREGRINUS

Tip

Unlike a planted framed garden, where all the plants must have similar needs, a variety of plants can be used for this project. We used a combination of colors, textures, and foliage sizes, not forgetting trailing plants! Whenever possible, allow approximately 1 inch (2.5cm) of space at the top of each pot. This will help to prevent soil from falling out when the plant sits tilted in the frame.

Supplies

· Tape measure or ruler

· Pencil

· 2 pieces of 1 inch x 3 inch x 6 foot (2.5cm x 7.5cm x 1.8m) common pine board

· 1 piece of 1 inch x 4 inch x 6 foot (2.5cm x 10cm x 1.8m) common pine board

· Chop saw (mitre saw)

· Jigsaw

· Nail gun and 18-gauge nails (1¼ inches [3cm] long)

· 6 potted plants in 4-inch (10cm) pots (plastic or terracotta)

· Hanging option of your choice (Command™ strips or picture-hanging kit)

To create a framed garden, you will need:

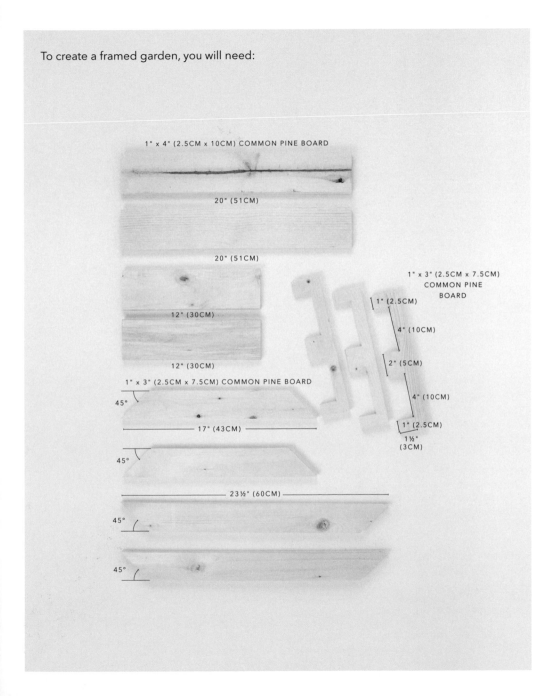

1" x 4" (2.5CM x 10CM) COMMON PINE BOARD

20" (51CM)

20" (51CM)

1" x 3" (2.5CM x 7.5CM)
COMMON PINE
BOARD

12" (30CM)

1" (2.5CM)

4" (10CM)

2" (5CM)

12" (30CM)

4" (10CM)

1" x 3" (2.5CM x 7.5CM) COMMON PINE BOARD

45°

1" (2.5CM)

17" (43CM)

1½"
(3CM)

45°

23½" (60CM)

45°

45°

Steps

1. Using the image shown on the previous page, measure and mark the pieces of pine board, then cut them out using the appropriate saw. Only three of the pieces will require the use of the jigsaw (the sawtooth pieces that will actually hold the pots).

2. Put together a box shape with the 1 x 4-inch (2.5cm x 10cm) pieces. The 12-inch (30cm) lengths are the top and bottom (horizontals) and the 20-inch (51cm) lengths are the sides (verticals). Note that the sides run long, and the top and bottom fit between them.

3. At each corner of both long pieces, nail through to the smaller piece to join them at each end point.

4. The pieces with the 45° angle ends create the frame that sits on top of the box. Start by laying one of these pieces down on the box. Be sure to line up the shorter side flush with the inside of the box.

5. Lay the other pieces out to center all the sides before nailing. Nail the first frame piece at each end to the box underneath. Repeat with the other three sides of the top frame.

6. Secure the four corners of the top frame by adding a nail through each corner into the adjoining piece.

7. The sawtooth pieces will hold the pots in place. Add the first one at the bottom of the box, with the teeth facing upward. Now tilt the teeth backward, keeping the back of the long edge flush with the box. The top of the teeth should be 1 inch (2.5cm) from the outside of the frame.

7

8

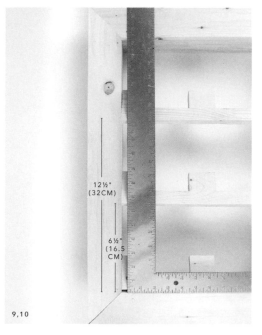

12½"
(32CM)

6½"
(16.5
CM)

9,10

8. Once at the correct angle (23°), nail through the box into the top teeth. This is tricky, because it's right below the frame, but you can do it! Use three nails on each side of the sawtooth piece to make sure it's secure. Repeat the nailing process on the other side of the first sawtooth piece.

9. Place the next sawtooth piece in the frame, 6½ inches (16.5cm) up from the bottom of the box, and repeat steps 7 and 8 for angling and nailing.

10. Place the final sawtooth piece in the frame, 12½ inches (32cm) from the bottom of the box, and repeat steps 7 and 8 for angling and nailing.

11. Add in your six potted plants!

Hanging your framed garden

Hanging techniques will vary depending on your situation. If you are renting or in an office where you're prohibited from making holes in the walls, a product such as heavy-duty Command™ strips can work very well. Be sure to use strips with a capacity of at least 10 lb (4.5kg) per strip. Use one strip set per corner of the framed garden and use as directed for best results. Add one plant at a time to test the weight limit. If you don't mind making holes in your walls and want to use a picture-hanging kit, we suggest buying one with a weight capacity of 30–40 lb (13–18kg). Follow the kit instructions in order to hang your framed garden.

Care

Water

Pull the pots out to water them as needed, and let them drip dry before placing them back in the frame. This helps to prevent moisture from reaching the walls.

CONSIDER ADDING POPS OF COLOR TO YOUR FRAMED GARDEN.

Houseplants 101 teaches us to group plants with similar care needs together. These indoor garden projects take that one step further to create unique statement-piece displays for your treasured collections.

INDOOR GARDENS

Indoor greenhouse

A few years ago, we shared a photo of a beautiful little indoor greenhouse on our @houseplantclub Instagram page, and it quickly became one of our most popular posts of all time. There was something about the golden light hitting the potted plants encased in glass that made a magical photo. Since then, indoor greenhouses have become increasingly popular among houseplant enthusiasts.

Whether you lack space, humidity, or adequate lighting elsewhere in your home, an indoor greenhouse may allow you to grow exciting plants that you otherwise wouldn't be able to, such as *Dischidia* and *Anthurium*. There are now entire social media accounts dedicated to sharing information about how best to build and maintain these timeless conservatories. While making your own glasshouse from scratch is possible, plenty of manufacturers offer them ready-made. IKEA has long been a favorite shopping destination for plant-lovers because of its foliage selection and plant product lines. These days, its glass cabinets, such as Detolf, Fabrikör, and Milsbo, are being transformed into greenhouses in homes around the world.

Paradoxically, indoor greenhouses have become so popular on sites such as Instagram and Pinterest that you can feel overwhelmed if you try to find the basic steps and information you need to modify one yourself. A vast array of sizes and styles are available commercially, but here we've selected a simple IKEA Fabrikör as our template. With help from friends such as Deanna (@habitpattern.sf) on Instagram, we've come up with some fairly simple modifications that will turn your cabinet into the greenhouse of your dreams. These steps are meant to get you started, so don't be afraid to make further modifications based on your home's requirements, or to venture down the internet rabbit hole looking for additional inspiration. Have fun filling your greenhouse with your favorite specimens, and be ready to talk about your work like the curator you are whenever you invite people over to your home.

AN ASSORTMENT OF HUMIDITY-LOVING PLANTS SUCH AS BEGONIAS, ORCHIDS, PHILODENDRON AND TRADESCANTIA FILL THE GREENHOUSE CABINET. DRACAENA ZEYLANICA BORROWS SOME OF THE GROW LIGHT'S STRENGTH FROM OUTSIDE THE CABINET.

Depending on where you live, the climate of your home, the plants you choose to grow, and the light level where you place your cabinet, you may not need things such as grow lights for brightness or pebble trays/ humidifiers for added humidity.

Supplies

· Suitable cabinet/indoor greenhouse

· 2-inch (5cm) hole saw and blade-oating lubricant

· 2-inch (5cm) plastic grommet

· Weatherstripping

· LED grow-light strips

· Heavy-duty double-sided tape

· Zip ties/cable ties

· Small fans (one for each shelf; the kind that are used for cooling electronics are best)

· Power strip

· Acrylic trays (to create pebble trays for added humidity)

· Small pebbles (enough to fill the acrylic trays about halfway)

· Humidifier

· Acrylic risers

· Suction cups with hooks

· Magnetic hooks

· Other decorative items (optional)

Steps

1. To get electrical wiring into your greenhouse, you will need to cut a hole in the bottom shelf, ideally before assembling it. Decide which side of the cabinet you want the wires to emerge from, and use the hole saw to drill a 2-inch (5cm) hole in the base, using enough lubricant to keep the cut smooth. Place the grommet in the hole, to protect the wires from rubbing against bare metal and to prevent your greenhouse from losing moisture.

2. Now assemble your greenhouse, if necessary, following the manufacturer's instructions.

3. Close off any gaps between glass and metal with weatherstripping, following the directions on the packaging.

4. If your home does not have a bright enough place for your chosen plants, you'll need to install grow lights. There are numerous types, and many have several brightness settings. For cabinets that are not placed in a brightly lit area, we recommend adding one or two strips of LED grow lights per shelf. They usually come with heavy-duty double-sided tape to adhere them to the cabinet, but you may want to swap it for clear tape strips that will be less conspicuous.

5. Feed the wires through the hole in the base of the cabinet. Fabrikör has a small metal lip under the base where you can hide all your wires away using zip ties/cable ties and heavy-duty double-sided tape. Plug them into a power strip underneath the cabinet.

6. Adding a pebble tray to one or more shelves may become important in drier climates or in the winter, when central heating dries out the

air inside your home. Half-fill an acrylic tray with pebbles and top up with water, which will evaporate slowly inside the greenhouse, increasing the moisture in the air around the plants. Alternatively, use a humidifier.

7. Once you have set your cabinet up, it's time to fill it with your favorite specimens. You can use the acrylic risers to create different levels for your plants. Mounted plants can be hung from suction cups, and heavy-duty magnetic hooks can support small hanging items on the top shelf.

8. Think about what else might look great under bright lights; maybe add a hanging prism or a radiometer. Mix in different colors and textures, and think about how your indoor greenhouse can become your own little botanical museum.

Care

With so many variables including daylight, supplemental lighting, pebble trays, fans, and the plants themselves, you may find that you have to adjust things to achieve the best growing environment. As with all plant set-ups, it's important to observe and learn the signs of unhappiness in your plants, so that you can work out how to treat them.

Water

Humidity should be maintained above 70 percent for tropical species. To avoid condensation on surfaces, which may result in mold, aim for a humidity level somewhere between 70 and 90 percent, monitoring it using a thermometer with temperature and humidity readings. Pay attention to how the temperature and humidity change throughout the year, because as temperatures drop, less water vapor is needed to maintain higher humidity.

Light

You may be able to avoid using supplemental lighting altogether if you place your greenhouse cabinet in a well-lit space. The goal is to mimic the lighting in each plant's natural environment. For tropicals, this means bright light for several hours a day.

HARVEST THE POWER OF THE SUN BY PLACING YOUR GREENHOUSE NEAR A BRIGHT WINDOW AND YOU WON'T NEED TO COMPENSATE WITH GROW LIGHTS.

Propagation centerpiece

Propagating plants makes for beautiful home decor. We're going to show you how to make a lovely centerpiece to display your propagating plants using cement and glass. It's perfect for a dining table, coffee table, or fireplace mantle. You could use the centerpiece as decor at your next party, and you could even allow attendees to take home plant clippings. Simply remove the cutting from the centerpiece, wrap in a wet paper towel, and place in a baggie for transport home.

This centerpiece is made using five identical glass spice jars, spaced evenly in a row, set into cement. However, you can mix up the sizes of glass tube or jar if you prefer. We used about 5 lb (2.25kg) dry concrete to make our centerpiece, which is 1½ inches (3cm) thick and 18 inches (46cm) long. As with all projects, it is important to take safety precautions while working. We recommend wearing a mask, protective eyewear, and gloves when mixing concrete and using a saw.

MONSTERA ADANSONII

Supplies

Mold

· 1 inch x 4 inch x 6 foot (2.5cm x 10cm x 1.8m) pine common board

· Measuring tape

· Pencil

· Chop saw (or handsaw)

· Nail gun with 18-gauge nails (or a hammer and 18-gauge brad nails)

Centerpiece

· Painter's tape

· Cooking spray (coconut, avocado, or olive oil)

· Glass tubes (such as test tubes or spice jars)

· Quick-dry concrete (we used half of a 10-lb (4.5kg) bucket for one centerpiece)

· At least 1 gallon (3.75 liter) water, for mixing the concrete (you will not use it all)

· Mixing stick

· Putty knife

· Spirit level (optional)

· Hammer

· Sandpaper

Tip

Here we walk you through how to create a mold for the propagation centerpiece. But you could use plastic or cardboard to create your mold, or repurpose an item from around the house, such as an old plastic container or an ice-cream tub. If you choose to use something other than our mold, skip the mold-making section and start with the Centerpiece steps.

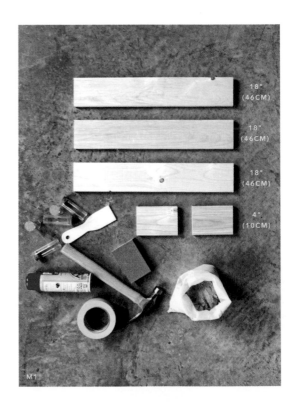

Steps

Mold
1. Measure out and mark the five pieces on the common board: you will need three pieces that are 18 inches (46cm) long, and two pieces that are 4 inches (10cm) long. Double-check your measurements before cutting the wood with the chop saw or handsaw.

2. Place one 18-inch (46cm) piece flat on your work surface. The other 18-inch (46cm) pieces will make up the sides. Nail the long sides to the base, using just one nail in each corner.

3. Next, nail one 4-inch (10cm) piece to the end of the mold using just one nail in each corner. Repeat at the other end to complete your mold.

Centerpiece
1. Use the painter's tape to cover any gaps in the mold so the concrete cannot leak through. Thoroughly tape the bottom 1 inch (2.5cm) of each glass tube.

2. Coat the inside of the mold with a thin layer of cooking spray, as well as the taped section of each glass tube, to lubricate.

3. Mix the concrete following the manufacturer's directions. The consistency should be similar to that of yogurt.

4. Pour the concrete into the mold and spread it evenly with the putty knife. Try to get it as level on the top as possible, since this is how it will dry.

5. Slowly push the jars down 1 inch (2.5cm) into the concrete, turning them as you do so. Be careful not to go all the way to the bottom.

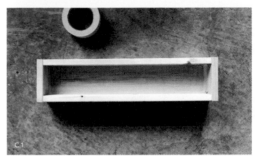

C10

C11

6. The cement should be thick enough that you don't have to hold the glass jars in place. However, do make sure they're sitting level in the concrete. We eyeballed the level of our jars, but you could use a spirit level.

7. As the concrete begins to dry, rotate the glass jars a few times every 5 minutes, to ensure they do not stick. This helps to create the place for the jar to sit, making it easy to move the jars in and out to replace water and plants.

8. After 20-30 minutes, the cement should be dry enough to remove the jars but still hold the jar shape without the hole collapsing. Remove the tape from the glass jars and wash them with soap and water ready for use in the centerpiece.

9. Allow the cement to dry overnight (just to be safe).

10. Use the hammer to break away the sides of the mold. The nails should come out and the wood should come off easily without ruining the concrete.

11. Use the sandpaper to smooth any cracks or sharp edges in the concrete.

12. Place the glass tubes back in the cement centerpiece and you're done!

STATIONS CAN BE MADE USING MANY MATERIALS, INCLUDING CEMENT OR WOOD.

Planted side table

We all know that we can place a potted plant *on top* of a side table, but have you ever considered placing a plant *inside* a side table? If you aim to live surrounded by botanicals, this is one way to incorporate plants into your decor in a novel way. This project can be put together very quickly once you have procured your plants and selected a suitable side table. Make sure you find one with a tray—preferably removable—that is at least 1 inch (2.5cm) deep. The table pictured here is 20 inches (50cm) tall, and has a tray 1¼ inches (3cm) deep and 14 inches (35cm) wide. Your table should be made of an impermeable material (such as metal or glass) that can hold several pounds of soil, plants, and rocks, and stand up to contact with moisture from time to time.

ADDING DIFFERENTLY-SIZED CACTI AND
SUCCULENTS BRINGS VISUAL INTEREST
TO THE PLANTED SIDE TABLE.

Supplies

· Tarp or sheets of newsprint

· Stainless-steel side table with tray

· Activated charcoal

· Potting soil

· Gardening gloves

· Small plants

· Decorative rocks

<u>Steps</u>

1. Spread a layer of activated charcoal in the bottom of the tray. This will absorb excess moisture and help to prevent rot.

2. Add a thin layer of potting soil on top of the charcoal layer.

3. Wearing gardening gloves, remove the plants from their pots and gently massage the roots until they are able to be spread out and flattened. Begin planting in the center of the table, placing the tallest plants there and moving out toward the edges with squatter and shorter plants. Fill in the gaps with small cacti and succulents. Turn the tray as you go so that you put together a well-rounded grouping.

4. Once you have the plants where you want them, add decorative rocks to anchor them and cover the soil. For the project pictured here, we used 5 lb (2.25kg) of small white pebbles.

Tip
Working with cacti can be tricky! Protect yourself from unwanted pokes by handling the plants by the roots whenever possible. Alternatively, wear rubberized gardening gloves and use kitchen tongs to handle the plants, or wrap a few layers of newsprint around the cacti before touching them.

Care

Upkeep and maintenance of your planted table will depend on the specific plants you chose. Cacti and succulents are great choices for this project because they have shallow roots and thrive in dry soil.

Water
One of the things we always stress is to ensure proper drainage in any container, but obviously that won't work here (once you know the rules, you can break them!). Because of this, be very mindful of the amount of water you add to the planted table. Succulents and cacti store water in their cells, which is why they look so plump when well watered. They tend to sag and even wrinkle when in need of a drink. It's very important that you add water to the soil mix sparingly to ensure that none of the plants develops root rot.

Light
Make sure your table is placed in a well-lit spot near a bright window.

A well-planted room is imaginative and artistic while remaining grounded in the natural world. Plants allow for endless creative possibilities when paired with a willing creator, some basic materials, and a little bit of elbow grease.

THE PLANTED ROOM

Levels and groups

Take advantage of differing light levels by placing plants in brighter or shadier places within a room. Group pieces with similar care needs together to keep tending to your plants manageable.

Shelfie style

Give us a shelf in a sunny room and we will undoubtedly place a trailing plant on it. But don't stop there—plants love friends and shelves are a great way to display your favorites.

More ways with walls

When you've run out of floor space, look to the walls for inspiration. This is a great opportunity to repurpose a found item or make something unique that is all your own.

Sideboard displays

Take advantage of furniture around your home that can double as an oversized plant stand. Whether it's a few select small plants or an entire mini jungle, you can turn your furniture into one big statement piece.

The maximalist room

Throw the rules out of the door! When it comes to maximalist plant decor, the sky is actually the limit. With plants on the floor, tabletops, walls, and ceilings, you're literally bringing the outdoors in.

Pick a favorite

Some of us are partial to specific plant species. Whether you are a fan of the Fiddle Leaf Fig or the whole Philodendron family, displaying several together can make for a striking scene.

More ways to hang

Whether you have a favorite fiber artist or you're a DIYer, there's a unique plant hanger for you. Group together different colors, lengths, and styles to create a cool, breezy, laid-back feel in your home.

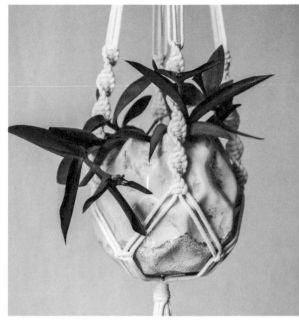

Water beauties

Propagating plants in water can be fun and rewarding but it can also be a way to accessorize your home decor. With different sized plants and vessels, the possibilities are endless.

About the authors

Morgan Doane lives in Tampa, Florida, with her husband Brian and their 16-year-old dog, Foster. Her love of plants and their pots inspired her to learn ceramics and she now proudly makes pieces every day in her home studio. She enjoys bird-watching, kayaking, and traveling when she isn't covered in potting soil or wet clay. You can follow her adventures on Instagram at @plantingpink.

Erin Harding lives just outside of Portland, Oregon, with her husband Tim and their boys, Oliver and Otis. Erin enjoys spreading the plant love and inspiration through in-person workshops, blogging at cleverbloom.com, and sharing planty pics on Instagram. On the weekends she loves to drink coffee, go plant shopping, and spend time with her family.

Acknowledgments

Writing a project-based book in the middle of a pandemic is definitely not easy. A huge thank you to our super husbands, Brian Doane and Tim Harding, who both played so many different roles, including designers, builders, and plant haulers. Further thanks go to Nate Meeds who risked the virus to capture just the right shots with us in a small studio. To Cory Paul Jarrell for supplying locally grown plants for our projects. To Oliver and Otis Harding for being our biggest fans! Lastly, we want to thank our editors Zara Larcombe and Chelsea Edwards for working with us through what was likely the hardest year of our lives on a book that we are now incredibly proud to have finished.

Picture credits

Unless otherwise stated, all images by Morgan Doane and Erin Harding.

The authors would like to thank the following for kindly providing images for this book:

2 Image styled and photographed by Rebecca deBarros @ellemenoh.plants, Propagation stations created by Dimitri Tsimikas @dimitritsimikas; 13 left Charmaine Adrina @unplantparenthood; 13 right Brooklyn Akins @vora.brook @vora.beauty; 14 Brad Canning from leafy lane @leafy.lane; 15 Tash Soumalias @indoorplantfamily; 18 above Photo: Jesse Waldman for @pistilsnursery; 44 above Photo: Irene Malasidou - The Pot Founder; 46, 47 Photos by Regula Roost for Green Bubble, greenbubble.ch; 63, 67, 74 Photo Jesse Waldman for @pistilsnursery; 69 onurdongel/Getty Images; 75 Thanate Rooprasert/Shutterstock; 82 Cecilia Möller/living4media; 83 above & below, Aya @living_lush_life; 85, 89 Cooper&Smith Propagation Stations. Photo by Brayden Smith @bcsimaging; 96 Ekaterina Khudyakova/EyeEm/Getty Images; 97 above left Evelyn Sisco @greenwithevy; 97 above right Cyril Cybernated @cyrilcybernated; 97 below Westend61/Getty Images; 98 Lex @plantsaturated; 99 above left Piyanut Sirikate/Shutterstock; 99 below DorotaSe/Shutterstock; 100 Jillian Cain Photography/Shutterstock; 101 left Styled by Lauren Casel @mylittlegreenapt; 101 right Dayna Friedman @elvysweethome; 102 Dorina Verdyck, Plant&Stek; 103 above left @sisiliareads; 103 above right Gergely Nemeth @eliotparke Frank Schroder @frankyfolia (kitchen cabinet Berlin, May 2020); 103 below left Lindsay Wallstrum @leafandlolo; 103 bottom right @seth_blackk; 104 Chad Kemper/Alamy Stock Photo; 105 Seija @plantsandcollecting; 107 above left Dorrington Reid; 107 above right Monie Darlington @flora_and_furnish; 107 below Josh McCarthy @the_foxandlion & @electricityscape_photo Web: www.electricityscape.com.au; 108 Kristien Verreydt, "Hanging plant" - originally shared on Instagram by Projectfivetonine Source: https://www.instagram.com/p/CEYdoPXDHnO/; 109 above left & right Courtesy of Ekaterina Aleksandrova, Evening Sun Macrame, @esmacrame; 109 below Evelyn Sisco @greenwithevy; 110 Jenna Boholij @jbird_photos; 111 above left Mint Images/Shutterstock; 111 above right & below @noponlyplants @digitaltomato.

Photography by Nate Meeds on pages 6-7, 10, 12, 16-17, 19, 22-27, 30-31, 34-39, 42-43, 44 below - 45, 48-54, 57, 59, 64-65, 68, 70-73, 81, 84, 86-88, 90-93